Key Facts™ on

Oman

~*Essential Information on Oman*~

By Patrick W. Nee

The Internationalist®

www.internationalist.com

The Internationalist®

International Business, Investment, and Travel

Published by:

The Internationalist Publishing Company

96 Walter Street/ Suite 200

Boston, MA 02131, USA

Tel: 617-354-7722

www.internationalist.com

PN@internationalist.com

Copyright © 2013 by PWN

Table Of Contents

Chapter 1: Background

The inhabitants of the area of Oman have long prospered on Indian Ocean trade. In the late 18th century, a newly established sultanate in Muscat signed the first in a series of friendship treaties with Britain. Over time, Oman's dependence on British political and military advisors increased, but it never became a British colony. In 1970, QABOOS bin Said Al-Said overthrew his father, and he has since ruled as sultan. His extensive modernization program has opened the country to the outside world while preserving the longstanding close ties with the UK. Oman's moderate, independent foreign policy has sought to maintain good relations with all Middle Eastern countries. Inspired by the popular uprisings that swept the Middle East and North Africa beginning in January 2011, Omanis began staging marches and demonstrations to demand economic benefits, an end to corruption, and greater political rights. In response to protester demands, QABOOS in 2011 pledged to implement economic and political reforms, such as granting legislative and regulatory powers to the Majlis al-Shura and introducing unemployment benefits. In August 2012, the Sultan announced a royal directive mandating the speedy implementation of a national job creation plan for thousands of public and private sector jobs. As part of the government's efforts to decentralize authority and allow greater citizen participation in local governance, Oman successfully conducted its first municipal council elections in December 2012. Announced by the Sultan in 2011, the municipal councils will have the power to advise the Royal Court on the needs of local districts across Oman's 11 governorates.

Chapter 2: Geography

Location:

Middle East, bordering the Arabian Sea, Gulf of
Oman, and Persian Gulf, between Yemen and UAE

Geographic coordinates:

21 00 N, 57 00 E

Map references:

Middle East

Area:

total: 309,500 sq km

country comparison to the world: 71

land: 309,500 sq km

water: 0 sq km

Area - comparative:

slightly smaller than Kansas

Land boundaries:

total: 1,374 km

border countries: Saudi Arabia 676 km, UAE 410 km,
Yemen 288 km

Coastline:

2,092 km

Maritime claims:

territorial sea: 12 nm

contiguous zone: 24 nm

exclusive economic zone: 200 nm

Climate:

dry desert; hot, humid along coast; hot, dry interior; strong southwest summer monsoon (May to September) in far south

Terrain:

central desert plain, rugged mountains in north and south

Elevation extremes:

lowest point: Arabian Sea 0 m

highest point: Jabal Shams 2,980 m

Natural resources:

petroleum, copper, asbestos, some marble, limestone, chromium, gypsum, natural gas

Land use:

arable land: 0.1%

permanent crops: 0.12%

other: 99.77% (2011)

Irrigated land:

588.5 sq km (2004)

Total renewable water resources:

1.4 cu km (2011)

Freshwater withdrawal (domestic/industrial/agricultural):

> total: 1.32 cu km/yr (10%/1%/88%)
>
> per capita: 515.8 cu m/yr (2003)

Natural hazards:

> summer winds often raise large sandstorms and dust storms in interior; periodic droughts

Environment - current issues:

> rising soil salinity; beach pollution from oil spills; limited natural freshwater resources

Environment - international agreements:

> party to: Biodiversity, Climate Change, Climate Change-Kyoto Protocol, Desertification, Hazardous Wastes, Law of the Sea, Marine Dumping, Ozone Layer Protection, Ship Pollution, Whaling
>
> signed, but not ratified: none of the selected agreements

Geography - note:

> strategic location on Musandam Peninsula adjacent to Strait of Hormuz, a vital transit point for world crude oil

Chapter 3: People and Society

Nationality:

noun: Omani(s)

adjective: Omani

Ethnic groups:

Arab, Baluchi, South Asian (Indian, Pakistani, Sri Lankan, Bangladeshi), African

Languages:

Arabic (official), English, Baluchi, Urdu, Indian dialects

Religions:

Ibadhi Muslim (official) 75%, other (includes Sunni Muslim, Shia Muslim, Hindu) 25%

Population:

3,154,134 (July 2013 est.)

country comparison to the world: 136

note: includes 577,293 non-nationals

Age structure:

0-14 years: 30.6% (male 494,444/female 469,752)

15-24 years: 20.2% (male 333,583/female 302,618)

25-54 years: 42.1% (male 781,396/female 547,872)

55-64 years: 3.9% (male 65,722/female 56,673)

<u>65 years and over</u>: 3.2% (male 51,515/female 50,559) (2013 est.)

Median age:

<u>total</u>: 24.7 years

<u>male</u>: 25.9 years

<u>female</u>: 23.1 years (2013 est.)

Population growth rate:

2.06% (2013 est.)

<u>country comparison to the world</u>: 48

Birth rate:

24.43 births/1,000 population (2013 est.)

<u>country comparison to the world</u>: 61

Death rate:

3.4 deaths/1,000 population (2013 est.)

<u>country comparison to the world</u>: 216

Net migration rate:

-0.47 migrant(s)/1,000 population (2013 est.)

<u>country comparison to the world</u>: 133

Urbanization:

<u>urban population</u>: 73.4% of total population (2011)

<u>rate of urbanization</u>: 2.23% annual rate of change (2010-15 est.)

Major urban areas - population:

MUSCAT (capital) 634,000 (2009)

Sex ratio:

at birth: 1.05 male(s)/female

0-14 years: 1.05 male(s)/female

15-24 years: 1.1 male(s)/female

25-54 years: 1.45 male(s)/female

55-64 years: 1.17 male(s)/female

65 years and over: 1.03 male(s)/female

total population: 1.22 male(s)/female (2013 est.)

Maternal mortality rate:

32 deaths/100,000 live births (2010)

country comparison to the world: 121

Infant mortality rate:

total: 14.46 deaths/1,000 live births

country comparison to the world: 115

male: 14.76 deaths/1,000 live births

female: 14.15 deaths/1,000 live births (2013 est.)

Life expectancy at birth:

total population: 74.72 years

country comparison to the world: 105

male: 72.84 years

female: 76.7 years (2013 est.)

Total fertility rate:

2.86 children born/woman (2013 est.)

country comparison to the world: 68

Contraceptive prevalence rate:

31.7% (2000)

Health expenditures:

2.8% of GDP (2010)

country comparison to the world: 181

Physicians density:

1.9 physicians/1,000 population (2008)

Hospital bed density:

1.8 beds/1,000 population (2009)

Drinking water source:

improved:

urban: 93% of population

rural: 78% of population

total: 89% of population

unimproved:

urban: 7% of population

rural: 22% of population

total: 11% of population (2010 est.)

Sanitation facility access:

improved:

urban: 100% of population

rural: 95% of population

total: 99% of population

unimproved:

urban: 0% of population

rural: 5% of population

total: 1% of population (2010 est.)

HIV/AIDS - adult prevalence rate:

0.1% (2009 est.)

country comparison to the world: 153

HIV/AIDS - people living with HIV/AIDS:

1,100 (2009 est.)

country comparison to the world: 138

HIV/AIDS - deaths:

fewer than 100 (2009 est.)

country comparison to the world: 116

Obesity - adult prevalence rate:

20.9% (2008)

country comparison to the world: 94

Children under the age of 5 years underweight:

8.6% (2009)

country comparison to the world: 72

Education expenditures:

4.3% of GDP (2009)

country comparison to the world: 102

Literacy:

definition: age 15 and over can read and write

total population: 81.4%

male: 86.8%

female: 73.5% (2003 census)

School life expectancy (primary to tertiary education):

total: 14 years

male: 14 years

female: 14 years (2011)

Chapter 4: Government and Key Leaders

Country name:

conventional long form: Sultanate of Oman

conventional short form: Oman

local long form: Saltanat Uman

local short form: Uman

former: Muscat and Oman

Government type:

monarchy

Capital:

name: Muscat

geographic coordinates: 23 37 N, 58 35 E

time difference: UTC+4 (9 hours ahead of
Washington, DC during Standard Time)

Administrative divisions:

11 governorates (muhafazat, singular - muhafazat);
Ad Dakhiliyah, Al Buraymi, Al Wusta, Az Zahirah,
Janub al Batinah (Al Batinah South), Janub ash
Sharqiyah (Ash Sharqiyah South), Masqat (Muscat),
Musandam, Shamal al Batinah (Al Batinah North),
Shamal ash Sharqiyah (Ash Sharqiyah North), Zufar
(Dhofar)

Independence:

1650 (expulsion of the Portuguese)

National holiday:

Birthday of Sultan QABOOS, 18 November (1940)

Constitution:

none; note - on 6 November 1996, Sultan QABOOS issued a royal decree promulgating a basic law considered by the government to be a constitution which, among other things, clarifies the royal succession, provides for a prime minister, bars ministers from holding interests in companies doing business with the government, establishes a bicameral legislature, and guarantees basic civil liberties for Omani citizens

Legal system:

mixed legal system of Anglo-Saxon law and Islamic law

International law organization participation:

has not submitted an ICJ jurisdiction declaration; non-party state to the ICCt

Suffrage:

21 years of age; universal; note - members of the military and security forces by law are not allowed to vote

Executive branch:

chief of state: Sultan and Prime Minister QABOOS bin Said Al-Said (sultan since 23 July 1970 and prime minister since 23 July 1972); note - the monarch is both the chief of state and head of government

head of government: Sultan and Prime Minister QABOOS bin Said Al-Said (sultan since 23 July 1970 and prime minister since 23 July 1972)

cabinet: Cabinet appointed by the monarch

elections: the Ruling Family Council determines a successor from the Sultan's extended family; if the Council cannot form a consensus within three days of the Sultan's death or incapacitation, the Defense Council will relay a predetermined heir as chosen by the Sultan

Legislative branch:

bicameral - consists of Majlis al-Dawla or upper chamber (71 seats; members appointed by the sultan; has only advisory powers) and Majlis al-Shura or lower chamber (84 seats; members elected by popular vote to serve four-year terms; body has authority to draft legislation but is subordinate to the Sultan)

elections: (Majlis al-Shura) last held on 15 October 2011 (next to be held in October 2015) election results: percent of vote by party - NA; seats by party - NA; note - three prominent figures from the Arab Spring 2011 protests won seats; one woman also won a seat

Judicial branch:

highest court(s): Supreme Court (consists of 5 judges)

judge selection and term of office: judges nominated by the 9-member Supreme Judicial Council (chaired by the monarch) and appointed by the monarch; judge tenure NA

subordinate courts: Courts of Appeal; Courts of First Instance; sharia courts; magistrates' courts

Political parties and leaders:

political parties are illegal

Political pressure groups and leaders:

International organization participation:

ABEDA, AFESD, AMF, CAEU, FAO, G-77, GCC, IAEA, IBRD, ICAO, ICC (NGOs), IDA, IDB, IFAD, IFC, IHO, ILO, IMF, IMO, IMSO, Interpol, IOC, IPU, ISO, ITSO, ITU, LAS, MIGA, NAM, OIC, OPCW, UN, UNCTAD, UNESCO, UNIDO, UNWTO, UPU, WCO, WFTU (NGOs), WHO, WIPO, WMO, WTO

Diplomatic representation in the US:

chief of mission: Ambassador Hunaina bint Sultan
bin Ahmad al-MUGHAIRI

chancery: 2535 Belmont Road, NW, Washington, DC
20008

telephone: [1] (202) 387-1980

FAX: [1] (202) 745-4933

Diplomatic representation from the US:

chief of mission: Ambassador Greta C. HOLTZ

embassy: Jamait Ad Duwal Al Arabiyya Street, Al
Khuwair area, Muscat

mailing address: P. O. Box 202, P.C. 115, Madinat Al
Sultan Qaboos, Muscat

telephone: [968] 24-643-400

FAX: [968] 24-64-37-40

Key Leaders:

Sultan	QABOOS bin Said Al Said
Special Representative for His Majesty the Sultan	THUWAYNI bin Shihab Al Said
Prime Min.	QABOOS bin Said Al Said
Dep. Prime Min. for Cabinet Affairs	FAHD bin Mahmud Al Said
Min. of Agriculture	Fuad bin Jafar bin

	Muhammad al-SAJWANI
Min. of Awqaf & Religious Affairs	**Abdallah bin Muhammad bin Abdallah al-SALIMI**
Min. of Civil Service	**Khalid bin Umar bin Said al-MARHUN**
Min. of Commerce & Industry	**Ali bin Masud bin Ali al-SUNAIDI**
Min. of Defense	**QABOOS bin Said Al Said**
Min. of Diwan of the Royal Court	**KHALID bin Hilal bin Saud al-Busaidi**
Min. of Education	**Madiha bint Ahmad bin Nasir al-SHIBYANIYAN**
Min. of Environment & Climate Affairs	**Muhammad bin Salim bin Said al-TUBI**
Min. of Finance	**QABOOS bin Said Al Said**
Min. of Fisheries	**Muhammad bin Ali al-QATABI**
Min. of Foreign Affairs	**QABOOS bin Said Al Said**
Min. of Health	**Ali bin Muhammad bin MUSA,** *Dr.*
Min. of Heritage & Culture	**HAYTHIM bin Tariq Al Said**
Min. of Higher Education	**RAWYA bint Saud al-Busaidi**

Min. of Housing	**Muhammad bin Saif al-SHABIBI**
Min. of Information	**Hamad bin Muhammad al-RASHDI**
Min. of Interior	**HAMUD bin Faisal bin Said al-Busaidi**
Min. of Justice	**Abd al-Malik bin Abdallah bin Ali al-KHALILI**
Min. of Legal Affairs	**Abdallah bin Muhammad bin Said al-SAIDI**
Min. of Manpower	**Abdallah bin Nasser bin Abdallah al-BAKRI**
Min. of Oil & Gas	**Muhammad bin Hamad bin Sayf al-RUMHI**
Min. of Regional Municipalities & Water Resources	**Ahmad bin Abdallah bin Muhammad al-SHUHI**
Min. of the Royal Office	**Sultan bin Muhammad al-NUMANI,** *Gen.*
Min. of Social Development	**MUHAMMAD bin Said bin Said al-Kalbani**
Min. of Sports Affairs	**Saad bin Muhammad bin Said al-Mardhuf al-SAADI**

Min. of Tourism	**Ahmad bin Nasir bin Hamad al-MAHRAZI**
Min. of Transport & Communications	**Ahmad bin Muhammad bin Salim al-FUTAISI**
Min. of State & Governor, Muscat Region	**SAYID al-Mutasim bin Hamud al-Busaidi**
Min. of State & Governor, Dhofar Region	**MUHAMMAD BIN SULTAN bin Hamud al-Busaidi**
Min. Responsible for Defense Affairs	**BADR bin Saud bin Harib al-Busaidi**
Min. Responsible for Foreign Affairs	**YUSUF bin Alawi bin Abdallah**
Sec. Gen., Council of Ministers	**SHAYKH al-Fadhl bin Muhammad bin Ahmad al-Harthi**
Special Adviser to His Majesty	**Salim bin Abdallah al-GHAZALI**
Special Adviser to His Majesty for Culture	**Abd al-Aziz bin Muhammad al-RUWAS**
Special Adviser to His Majesty for Economic Planning Affairs	**Muhammad bin ZUBAYR**
Special Adviser to His	**SHABIB bin Taymur Al Said**

Majesty for Environmental Affairs	
Special Adviser to His Majesty for External Liaison	**Umar bin Abd al-Munim al-ZAWAWI**
Special Adviser to His Majesty for Security Affairs	**Abdallah bin Salih Khalfan al-HABSI,** *Lt. Gen.*
Governor, Central Bank of Oman	**QABOOS bin Said Al Said**
Executive Pres., Central Bank of Oman	**Hamud bin Sangur bin Hashim al-ZADJALI**
Ambassador to the US	**Hunaina bint Sultan bin Ahmad al-MUGHAIRI**
Permanent Representative to the UN, New York	**Lyutha bint Sultan bin Ahmad al-MUGHAIRI**

Flag description:

three horizontal bands of white, red, and green of equal width with a broad, vertical, red band on the hoist side; the national emblem (a khanjar dagger in its sheath superimposed on two crossed swords in scabbards) in white is centered near the top of the vertical band; white represents peace and prosperity, red recalls battles against foreign invaders, and green symbolizes the Jebel Akhdar (Green Mountains) and fertility

National symbol(s):

Khanjar dagger superimposed on two crossed swords

National anthem:

name: "Nashid as-Salaam as-Sultani" (The Sultan's Anthem)

lyrics/music: Rashid bin Uzayyiz al KHUSAIDI/James Frederick MILLS, arranged by Bernard EBBINGHAUS

note: adopted 1932; new words were written after QABOOS bin Said al Said gained power in 1970; the anthem was first performed by the band of a British ship as a salute to the Sultan during a 1932 visit to Muscat; the bandmaster of the HMS Hawkins was asked to write a salutation to the Sultan on the occasion of his visiting the ship

Chapter 5: Economy

Economy - overview:

Oman is a middle-income economy that is heavily dependent on dwindling oil resources. Because of declining reserves and a rapidly growing labor force, Muscat has actively pursued a development plan that focuses on diversification, industrialization, and privatization, with the objective of reducing the oil sector's contribution to GDP to 9% by 2020 and creating more jobs to employ the rising numbers of Omanis entering the workforce. Tourism and gas-based industries are key components of the government's diversification strategy. However, increases in social welfare benefits, particularly since the Arab Spring, will challenge the government's ability to effectively balance its budget if oil revenues decline. By using enhanced oil recovery techniques, Oman succeeded in increasing oil production, giving the country more time to diversify, and the increase in global oil prices through 2011 provided the government greater financial resources to invest in non-oil sectors. In 2012, continued surpluses resulting from sustained high oil prices and increased enhanced oil recovery allowed the government to maintain growth in social subsidies and public sector job creation. However, the Sultan made widely reported statements indicating this would not be sustainable, and called for expanded efforts to support SME development and entrepreneurship. Government agencies and large oligarchic group companies heeded his call, announcing new initiatives to spin off non-essential functions to entrepreneurs, incubate new businesses, train and mentor up and coming business people, and provide financing for start-ups. In response to fast growth in household indebtedness, the Central Bank reduced the ceiling on personal interest loans from 8 to 7%, lowered mortgage rates, capped the percentage of consumer loans at 50% of borrower's salaries for personal loans and 60% for housing loans, and limited maximum repayment terms to 10 and 25 years respectively. In 2012 the Central Bank also issued final regulations governing Islamic banking and two full-fledged Islamic banks held oversubscribed IPOs while four traditional banks opened sharia-compliant Islamic windows.

GDP (purchasing power parity):

$91.54 billion (2012 est.)

country comparison to the world: 76

$87.16 billion (2011 est.)

$83.41 billion (2010 est.)

note: data are in 2012 US dollars

GDP (official exchange rate):

$76.46 billion (2012 est.)

GDP - real growth rate:

5% (2012 est.)

country comparison to the world: 65

4.5% (2011 est.)

5.6% (2010 est.)

GDP - per capita (PPP):

$29,600 (2012 est.)

country comparison to the world: 51

$29,100 (2011 est.)

$33,100 (2010 est.)

note: data are in 2012 US dollars

GDP - composition by sector:

agriculture: 1%

industry: 66%

services: 33% (2012 est.)

Labor force:

968,800

country comparison to the world: 142

: about 60% of the labor force is non-national (2007)

Labor force - by occupation:

agriculture: NA%

industry: NA%

services: NA%

Unemployment rate:

15% (2004 est.)

country comparison to the world: 145

Population below poverty line:

NA%

Household income or consumption by percentage share:

lowest 10%: NA%

highest 10%: NA%

Investment (gross fixed):

26.2% of GDP (2012 est.)

country comparison to the world: 42

Budget:

revenues: $36.36 billion

expenditures: $27.98 billion (2012 est.)

Taxes and other revenues:

47.6% of GDP (2012 est.)

country comparison to the world: 18

Budget surplus (+) or deficit (-):

11% of GDP (2012 est.)

country comparison to the world: 8

Public debt:

4.1% of GDP (2012 est.)

country comparison to the world: 153

4.6% of GDP (2011 est.)

Inflation rate (consumer prices):

2.9% (2012 est.)

country comparison to the world: 90

4.1% (2011 est.)

Central bank discount rate:

2% (31 December 2010 est.)

country comparison to the world: 143

0.05% (31 December 2009 est.)

Commercial bank prime lending rate:

5.65% (31 December 2012 est.)

country comparison to the world: 138

6.19% (31 December 2011 est.)

Stock of narrow money:

$9.083 billion (31 December 2012 est.)

country comparison to the world: 78

$7.971 billion (31 December 2011 est.)

Stock of broad money:

$71.42 billion (31 December 2010 est.)

$63.16 billion (31 December 2009 est.)

Stock of domestic credit:

$27.62 billion (31 December 2012 est.)

country comparison to the world: 73

$23.18 billion (31 December 2011 est.)

Market value of publicly traded shares:

$19.72 billion (31 December 2011)

country comparison to the world: 64

$20.27 billion (31 December 2010)

$17.3 billion (31 December 2009)

Agriculture - products:

dates, limes, bananas, alfalfa, vegetables; camels, cattle; fish

Industries:

crude oil production and refining, natural and liquefied natural gas (LNG) production; construction, cement, copper, steel, chemicals, optic fiber

Industrial production growth rate:

0.2% (2012 est.)

country comparison to the world: 130

Current account balance:

$10.22 billion (2012 est.)

country comparison to the world: 25

$10.67 billion (2011 est.)

Exports:

$52.04 billion (2012 est.)

country comparison to the world: 59

$47.09 billion (2011 est.)

Exports - commodities:

petroleum, reexports, fish, metals, textiles

Exports - partners:

China 31.9%, Japan 12.9%, UAE 10.1%, South Korea 10%, Thailand 4.4%, Singapore 4.4% (2012)

Imports:

$26.49 billion (2012 est.)

country comparison to the world: 68

$21.5 billion (2011 est.)

Imports - commodities:

machinery and transport equipment, manufactured goods, food, livestock, lubricants

Imports - partners:

UAE 23.6%, Japan 12.6%, India 8.5%, China 6.4%, US 6.1% (2012)

Reserves of foreign exchange and gold:

$14.75 billion (31 December 2012 est.)

country comparison to the world: 66

$14.37 billion (31 December 2011 est.)

Debt - external:

$10.18 billion (31 December 2012 est.)

country comparison to the world: 101

$9.297 billion (31 December 2011 est.)

Stock of direct foreign investment - at home:

$NA

Stock of direct foreign investment - abroad:

$NA

Exchange rates:

Omani rials (OMR) per US dollar:

0.3845 (2012 est.)

0.3845 (2011 est.)

0.3845 (2010 est.)

0.3845 (2009)

0.3845 (2008)

Fiscal year:

calendar year

Chapter 6: Energy

Electricity - production:

    18.59 billion kWh (2010 est.)

    country comparison to the world: 76

Electricity - consumption:

    15.34 billion kWh (2009 est.)

    country comparison to the world: 77

Electricity - exports:

    0 kWh (2010 est.)

    country comparison to the world: 106

Electricity - imports:

    0 kWh (2010 est.)

    country comparison to the world: 110

Electricity - installed generating capacity:

    4.202 million kW (2009 est.)

    country comparison to the world: 78

Electricity - from fossil fuels:

    100% of total installed capacity (2009 est.)

    country comparison to the world: 25

Electricity - from nuclear fuels:

    0% of total installed capacity (2009 est.)

    country comparison to the world: 143

Electricity - from hydroelectric plants:

0% of total installed capacity (2009 est.)

country comparison to the world: 185

Electricity - from other renewable sources:

0% of total installed capacity (2009 est.)

country comparison to the world: 161

Crude oil - production:

915,600 bbl/day (2012 est.)

country comparison to the world: 23

Crude oil - exports:

253,100 bbl/day (2012 est.)

country comparison to the world: 28

Crude oil - imports:

0 bbl/day (2009 est.)

country comparison to the world: 100

Crude oil - proved reserves:

4.902 billion bbl (1 January 2012 est.)

country comparison to the world: 26

Refined petroleum products - production:

106,000 bbl/day (2008 est.)

country comparison to the world: 72

Refined petroleum products - consumption:

98,000 bbl/day (2011 est.)

country comparison to the world: 80

Refined petroleum products - exports:

19,680 bbl/day (2008 est.)

country comparison to the world: 73

Refined petroleum products - imports:

33,150 bbl/day (2008 est.)

country comparison to the world: 85

Natural gas - production:

35.94 billion cu m (2012 est.)

country comparison to the world: 27

Natural gas - consumption:

17.53 billion cu m (2011 est.)

country comparison to the world: 38

Natural gas - exports:

11.49 billion cu m (2010 est.)

country comparison to the world: 21

Natural gas - imports:

1.9 billion cu m (2010 est.)

country comparison to the world: 51

Natural gas - proved reserves:

849.5 billion cu m (1 January 2012 est.)

country comparison to the world: 28

Carbon dioxide emissions from consumption of energy:

55.2 million Mt (2010 est.)

country comparison to the world: 58

Chapter 7: Communications

Telephones - main lines in use:

305,000 (2012)

country comparison to the world: 115

Telephones - mobile cellular:

5.278 million (2012)

country comparison to the world: 102

Telephone system:

general assessment: modern system consisting of
open-wire, microwave, and radiotelephone
communication stations; limited coaxial cable;
domestic satellite system with 8 earth stations

domestic: fixed-line and mobile-cellular
subscribership both increasing with fixed-line phone
service gradually being introduced to remote villages
using wireless local loop systems

international: country code - 968; the Fiber-Optic
Link Around the Globe (FLAG) and the SEA-ME-
WE-3 submarine cable provide connectivity to Asia,
the Middle East, and Europe; satellite earth stations -
2 Intelsat (Indian Ocean), 1 Arabsat (2008)

Broadcast media:

1 state-run TV broadcaster; TV stations transmitting from Saudi Arabia, the UAE, and Yemen available via satellite TV; state-run radio operates multiple stations; first private radio station began operating in 2007 and 2 additional stations now operating (2007)

Internet country code:

.om

Internet hosts:

14,531 (2012)

country comparison to the world: 127

Internet users:

1.465 million (2009)

country comparison to the world: 83

Chapter 8: Transportation

Airports:

    130 (2012)

    country comparison to the world: 43

Airports - with paved runways:

    total: 12

    over 3,047 m: 6

    2,438 to 3,047 m: 5

    914 to 1,523 m: 1 (2012)

Airports - with unpaved runways:

    total: 118

    over 3,047 m: 2

    2,438 to 3,047 m: 7

    1,524 to 2,437 m: 51

    914 to 1,523 m: 32

    under 914 m: 26 (2012)

Heliports:

    3 (2012)

Pipelines:

    condensate 106 km; gas 4,224 km; oil 3,558 km;

    oil/gas/water 33 km; refined products 264 km (2013)

Roadways:

    total: 45,985 km

country comparison to the world: 80

paved: 29,685 km (includes 1,384 km of
expressways)

unpaved: 16,300 km (2011)

Merchant marine:

total: 5

country comparison to the world: 125

by type: chemical tanker 1, passenger 1,
passenger/cargo 3

registered in other countries: 15 (Malta 5, Panama 10)
(2010)

Ports and terminals:

Mina' Qabus, Salalah, Suhar

Chapter 9: Military

Military branches:

Sultan's Armed Forces (SAF): Royal Army of Oman, Royal Navy of Oman, Royal Air Force of Oman (al-Quwwat al-Jawwiya al-Sultanat Oman) (2013)

Military service age and obligation:

18-30 years of age for voluntary military service; no conscription (2012)

Manpower available for military service:

males age 16-49: 985,957

females age 16-49: 737,812 (2010 est.)

Manpower fit for military service:

males age 16-49: 837,886

females age 16-49: 642,427 (2010 est.)

Manpower reaching militarily significant age annually:

male: 31,959

female: 30,264 (2010 est.)

Military expenditures:

11.4% of GDP (2005 est.)

country comparison to the world: 1

Chapter 10: Transnational Issues

Disputes - international:

boundary agreement reportedly signed and ratified with UAE in 2003 for entire border, including Oman's Musandam Peninsula and Al Madhah exclave, but details of the alignment have not been made public

Map of Oman

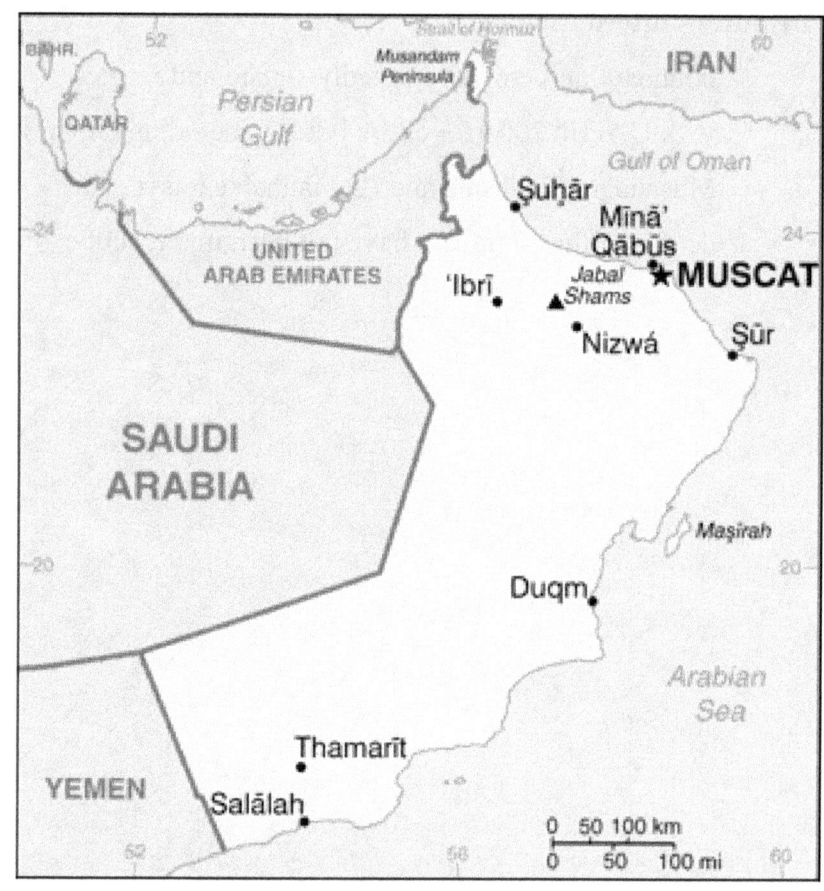

Other Key Facts™ Titles

Key Facts on South Korea

Key Facts on France

Key Facts on the United Kingdom

Key Facts on Egypt

Key Facts on Israel

Key Facts on Mexico

Key Facts on the United States of America

Key Facts on Turkey

Key Facts on South Africa

Key Facts on Greece

Key Facts on Japan

Key Facts on Malaysia

Key Facts on Vietnam

Key Facts on Hong Kong

Key Facts on Jordan

Key Facts on Australia

Key Facts on Venezuela

Key Facts on Canada

Key Facts on Burma (Myanmar)

Key Facts on Myanmar (Burma)

Key Facts on Singapore

Key Facts on Ireland

Key Facts on The Philippines

Key Facts on Thailand

Key Facts on Yemen

Key Facts on Bahrain

Key Facts on Kuwait

Key Facts on Lebanon

All Key Facts™ Titles are Available at

www.Amazon.com

THE INTERNATIONALIST®

2013

WWW.INTERNATIONALIST.COM

www.ingramcontent.com/pod-product-compliance
Lightning Source LLC
Chambersburg PA
CBHW071543170526
45166CB00004B/1525